Finger Puppet
-F·U·N-

THOMASINA SMITH

LORENZ BOOKS
LONDON • NEW YORK • SYDNEY • BATH

First published in 1996 by Lorenz Books

Lorenz Books is an imprint of Anness Publishing Limited, 1 Boundary Row, London SE1 8HP

© 1996 Anness Publishing Limited
Distributed in Canada by Raincoast Books Limited

ISBN 1 85967 321 X

A CIP catalogue record for this book is available from the British Library.

Publisher: Joanna Lorenz
Senior Children's Books Editor: Sue Grabham
Assistant Editor: Sophie Warne
Photographer: John Freeman
Designer: Michael R. Carter

Printed in China

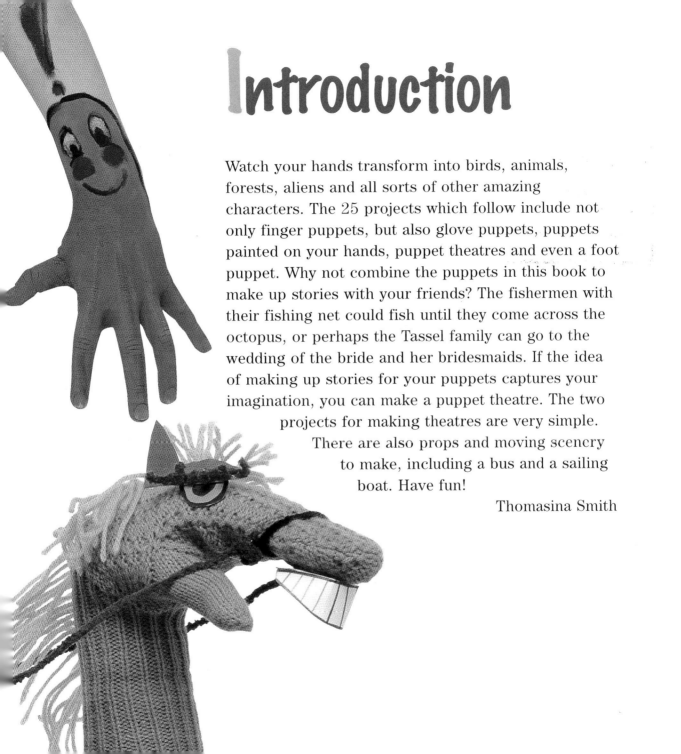

Introduction

Watch your hands transform into birds, animals, forests, aliens and all sorts of other amazing characters. The 25 projects which follow include not only finger puppets, but also glove puppets, puppets painted on your hands, puppet theatres and even a foot puppet. Why not combine the puppets in this book to make up stories with your friends? The fishermen with their fishing net could fish until they come across the octopus, or perhaps the Tassel family can go to the wedding of the bride and her bridesmaids. If the idea of making up stories for your puppets captures your imagination, you can make a puppet theatre. The two projects for making theatres are very simple. There are also props and moving scencry to make, including a bus and a sailing boat. Have fun!

Thomasina Smith

Contents

Materials

GLOVES AND SOCKS

Gloves and socks are a great starting point when making hand puppets, and mittens make ideal animal glove puppets. The finger and thumb parts of the mitten make a good snout and mouth. Gloves and socks come in all sorts of different materials – rubber, lace, wool, nylon – so keep an eye out!

WOODEN SKEWER

You can find wooden skewers in kitchen and hardware stores. They are sometimes sold as barbeque sticks. They have sharp ends, so don't forget to trim them with a pair of scissors. You can also use garden sticks, which are made to prop up plants, but they are not as easy to cut.

WOOL

Wool is ideal for making hair, and is good for stitching cut edges. Buy thick wool and hold onto any scraps, which may be useful for some of the other projects.

PIPE CLEANERS

You can buy pipe cleaners in craft and toy shops. There are many different colours and designs to choose from. Look out for brightly coloured, stripy and tinselly ones.

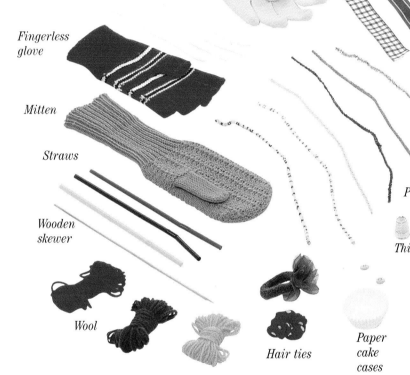

Washing-up glove

Lacy glove

Fingerless glove

Mitten

Straws

Wooden skewer

Wool

Hair ties

Paper cake cases

Thi...

THIMBLE

Always protect your fingers with a thimble when you are using a needle.

HAIR TIES

Hair ties come in a wide variety of shapes and colours from any chemist shop. They make good puppet hats and decorative extras. They are easy to use, as they are elasticated and will fit any finger size.

PAPER CAKE CASES

Traditionally used for making fairy cakes, paper cake cases can be bought in bright colours as well as the standard white ones.

NET

Nylon net is reasonably priced and easy to use because it doesn't fray when cut. It is great to use for veils and underskirts.

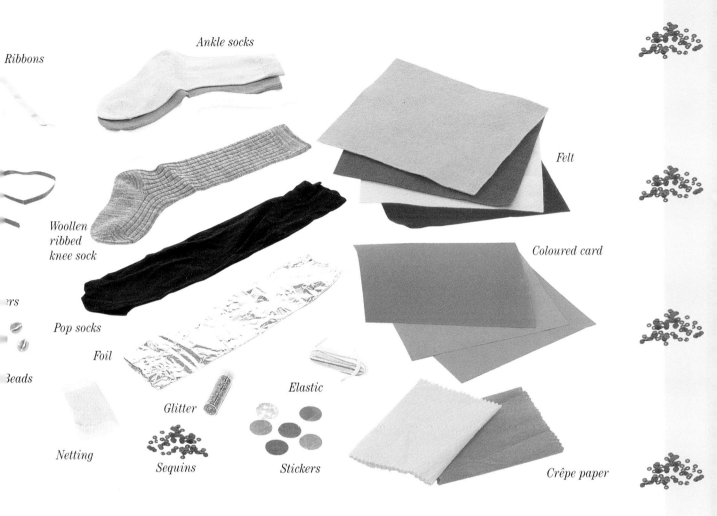

Ribbons

Ankle socks

Felt

Woollen ribbed knee sock

Pop socks

Coloured card

Foil

rs

Elastic

Beads

Glitter

Netting

Sequins

Stickers

Crêpe paper

GLITTER

Glitter adds sparkle to a finished puppet and is great for decorating. Loose glitter is sprinkled on top of glue and left to dry. It is good for large areas. Glitter glue sticks can be used for small areas.

ELASTIC

Elastic is sold in sewing shops. Ask for 5 mm to 10 mm widths.

STICKERS

Stickers are perfect for making facial features and decorating your puppets. Stationery shops sell sticker squares, circles and rectangles which can be cut into smaller shapes.

FELT

Felt doesn't fray when cut, so you can use it without having to sew the edges. It is also easy to draw on.

COLOURED CARD

Ask for card that can be cut easily with a pair of scissors, but which won't flop around. You may also need mount card, which is thicker and needs to be cut by an adult with a craft knife.

CREPE PAPER

Crêpe paper is like fabric because it bunches up and pleats beautifully.

Equipment

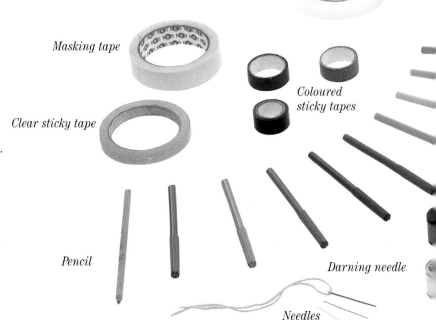

Double-sided sticky tape

Masking tape

Coloured sticky tapes

Clear sticky tape

Pencil

Darning needle

Needles

DOUBLE-SIDED STICKY TAPE

Double-sided sticky tape is clear sticky tape which is adhesive on both sides. It is perfect for sticking card and fabrics. Stick the tape to the surface and peel off the top layer of paper to uncover the other sticky side. It is very quick and neat to use.

MASKING TAPE

This paper tape is sticky on one side. It tears and peels off surfaces easily, and so is really only used for securing surfaces together while the glue is drying. It can then be taken off without leaving a mark.

COLOURED STICKY TAPE

You can find coloured sticky tape in electrical and hardware stores. It is good for decoration, but it doesn't always have very strong sticking power. Art and stationery shops have coloured sticky tapes that tend to be a lot stronger.

NEEDLES

When sewing with wool, use a large embroidery or darning needle. When sewing with fine thread, use a thin needle. Always wear a thimble to avoid pricking your fingers.

PAINT POT

You can buy paint pots in art or toy shops. The lid prevents your paint from drying out.

ACRYLIC AND POSTER PAINTS

Both acrylic paints and poster paints are water-based. They are very similar except that poster paints are less expensive and the colours aren't quite as strong as acrylic paints. Poster paints are adequate for painting finger puppets and puppet theatres.

PVA GLUE

Glue comes in many forms. PVA glue is also known as white glue and wood glue. It is white and comes in plastic bottles. You can pour some into a small bowl or put it in a paint pot. It is water-based, so it can easily be diluted with water if you don't need it too thick. Apply the glue with a glue brush. It takes a long time to dry, but when it is dry it is very strong and firm.

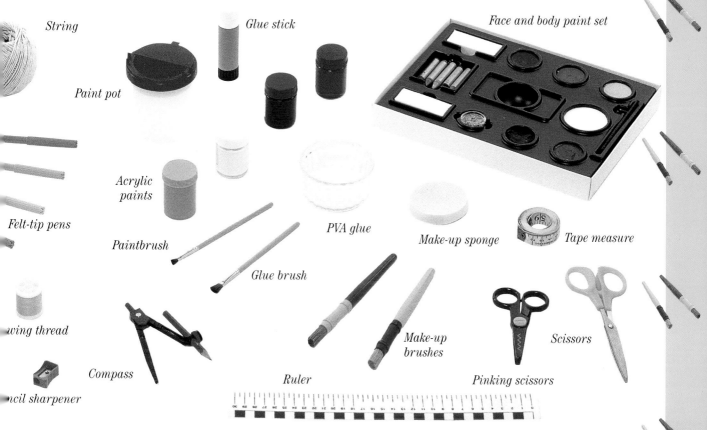

String

Glue stick

Face and body paint set

Paint pot

Acrylic paints

Felt-tip pens

Paintbrush

PVA glue

Make-up sponge

Tape measure

Glue brush

Make-up brushes

Scissors

_wing thread

Compass

Ruler

Pinking scissors

_ncil sharpener

GLUE STICKS

Glue sticks can be found in office, art and stationery shops. This is the best glue to use when sticking a flat sheet of paper onto a flat surface, as the paper rarely wrinkles or bubbles. Remember to replace the top after use as glue sticks dry up very quickly.

STATIONERY

A soft pencil, a ruler and a white rubber are the basic essentials of your craft equipment and are necessary for every project.

FACE AND BODY PAINTS

You can buy paint especially for painting face and hands. It washes off with water and doesn't irritate the skin. Try to buy a basic set that includes a make-up sponge, a make-up brush and make-up crayons, as well as a place to put water. Sometimes the brush supplied can be quite thin, so it is probably worth buying a second make-up brush, which you can find at the cosmetics counter of any chemist.

SCISSORS

If you can, it is a good idea to keep two pairs of scissors, one for fabric and one for paper. This prevents them from becoming blunt. Pinking scissors give you a zigzag edge and are really useful for decorating.

RULER

Some rulers measure only in centimetres or inches and some are marked with both. All the projects in this book use centimetres, so make sure that you have a suitable ruler.

Basic Techniques

One of the first techniques to master when making finger puppets is how to make a fabric or card tube for each finger. These tubes are the basis for your puppet characters.

FINGER TUBES

1 Cut a piece of card that is 7 cm wide and about 1 cm longer than your middle finger. Wrap it around your middle finger and trim the end.

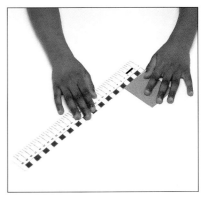

2 Measure the height of your card.

3 Draw five rectangles the same size as your test card.

4 Cut out the rectangles.

5 Stick a piece of double-sided sticky tape along one side edge of each card rectangle. Wrap the cards around your fingers and stick. Each finger will be slightly different.

6 Slot the puppet tubes onto your fingers and then decorate.

SEWING OR GLUING ONTO A SOCK

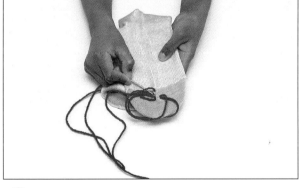

1 If you are decorating a sock or mitten, first draw the shape of the sock on a piece of thin card and cut it out. Make the shape slightly wider than the sock. Then slip the card into the sock to stretch it.

2 The card flattens the sock so that it is easier to work on. It also prevents you from sewing or gluing through to the other side of the sock!

Hand Painting

Use special face and body paints when painting on your hands, so that they won't irritate your skin. Always allow the paint to dry before applying a different colour – otherwise your masterpiece will become a mess!

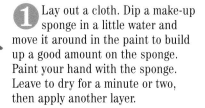

1 Lay out a cloth. Dip a make-up sponge in a little water and move it around in the paint to build up a good amount on the sponge. Paint your hand with the sponge. Leave to dry for a minute or two, then apply another layer.

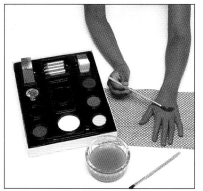

2 Use a brush to paint the details. Leave to dry before you use another colour.

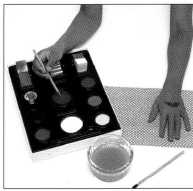

3 Have different bowls of water ready to clean the different colours from your brushes and sponges. Change the water if you have used it a lot.

12

Painting Features

By holding your hands in different positions you can make lots of shapes. There are all sorts of different effects to create, including a deer, a wolf and a footballer.

1 First apply the base paint. To make a mouth, pinch your thumb to the tips of your fingers.

2 Paint the hand in the clenched position first, then lay it out to relax it while you add more details.

13

Tassel Family

Here is a group of finger puppets with incredibly colourful hair made from tassels. On one hand is the Tassel family's mother and on the other hand sit her children. You can find suitable tassels in a shop that sells haberdashery.

YOU WILL NEED
Pair of lace gloves
Five medium tassels and
  one large tassel
Needle
Thread
Scissors
Crêpe paper
Ruler
Pinking scissors
Coloured card
Double-sided sticky tape
Felt-tip pen
Thin ribbon

14

1 Place the gloves in front of you with the palms facing upwards. On one glove, stitch the large tassel to the back of the middle finger to make the mother's hair. Sew the five smaller tassels to the fingertips of the other glove to make the children's hair.

2 Cut a rectangle of crêpe paper, measuring 7 cm by 20 cm. Gather up one long side so that it measures about 10 cm long. Using the pinking scissors, cut an apron from thin card and stick it to the middle of the crêpe paper with double-sided sticky tape. Stick the gathered edge of the crêpe paper to another piece of double-sided sticky tape. Do not peel the backing paper from the tape yet.

3 Draw and cut out six small circles from pink card to make the puppets' faces. Draw on the features using a felt-tip pen. Stick the faces onto the fingertips of the gloves using pieces of double-sided sticky tape.

4 Peel the backing from the double-sided sticky tape at the top of the crêpe paper skirt. Place the skirt sticky side up on your work surface. Press the mother puppet's glove onto the tape and wrap the skirt around the three middle fingers of the glove. Stick it on loosely enough to allow room for your fingers! Tie a length of thin ribbon around the mother's waist and the family is ready.

15

Woolly Jumper Gang

Fingerless woollen gloves make a great basis for a group of finger puppets wearing jumpers. Simply take another pair of gloves made from a thin fabric and slip them under the fingerless gloves. The gloved fingertips make the faces of your puppets. You can give each finger a different outfit.

YOU WILL NEED

Fingerless
  woollen glove
Buttons
Needle
Thread
Scissors
Felt
Ribbon
Coloured card
Felt-tip pen
Pair of thin gloves
  (lace or nylon)
PVA glue and glue brush
Hair ties

1 Slip your hand partly into a fingerless glove and carefully sew some buttons down the length of one of the fingers. Cut out a neck tie shape from a scrap of felt and sew it onto another finger. Sew a ribbon bow-tie onto another finger.

2 Cut out circles for faces from the coloured card and draw the features using a felt-tip pen.

3 Put on a thin glove and pull the fingerless glove over the top. Now pull both gloves off together in one go so that the thin glove stays inside the woolly one. Glue the faces onto the inner glove fingers and leave to dry.

4 Decorate a couple of your fingers with hair ties for hats.

Aliens

If you're into science fiction, why not make alien puppets for your fingers? These aliens have bodies made from silver kitchen foil that fits snugly over your hand. The aliens' faces are made from large and small paper stickers in very bright colours and they have long antennae to pick up radar signals.

YOU WILL NEED

Scissors
Kitchen foil
Clear sticky tape
Tinsel pipe cleaners
Ruler
Stickers
Felt-tip pen

1 Cut out five rectangles of foil just larger than your fingers, and wrap a piece around each finger. Fasten the foil with plenty of clear sticky tape so that the foil fingers are strong and don't rip. Now cut a rectangle of kitchen foil to cover your hand. Remember that you will need less on the thumb side of your hand.

2 Wrap your hand in the kitchen foil and cover with clear sticky tape. You will probably need several layers to seal any cracks.

3 Cut several pipe cleaners into 5 cm lengths. With your palm facing up, carefully tape two pipe cleaner pieces to each finger with clear sticky tape.

18

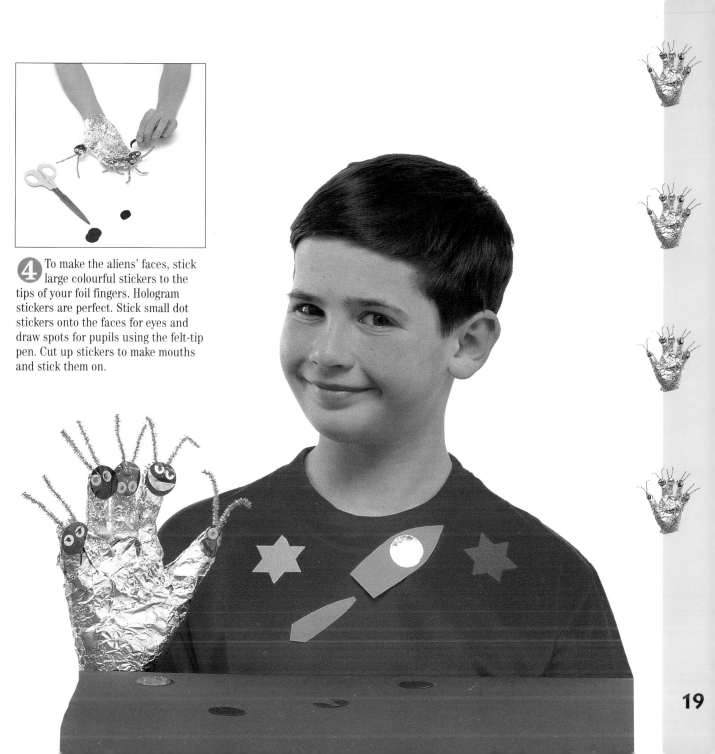

4 To make the aliens' faces, stick large colourful stickers to the tips of your foil fingers. Hologram stickers are perfect. Stick small dot stickers onto the faces for eyes and draw spots for pupils using the felt-tip pen. Cut up stickers to make mouths and stick them on.

Flower Fingers

This garden of flowers is really easy to make and is bright and colourful. Paper cake cases make great petals – buy coloured ones or paint white ones for yourself.

YOU WILL NEED

Scissors
Coloured card
Ruler
Pencil
Double-sided sticky tape
Paper cake cases
Acrylic paints
Paintbrushes
PVA glue and glue brush

20

1 Cut a piece of green card and make a tube to fit around your middle finger. Measure this card, then draw and cut out 10 pieces of card the same size. Stick a piece of double-sided sticky tape along the side edge of each card rectangle.

2 Peel off the paper from the back of the double-sided tape and roll up the tubes to fit each finger before sticking.

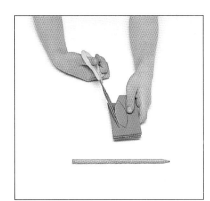

3 Fold a piece of green card into a concertina of 10 layers. Draw a leaf shape on the top and cut it out. This is a quick way of making all your leaves the same size.

4 If you are using white cake cases, paint them different colours. Cut out circles of coloured card and glue them in the bottoms of the cake cases to make the centres of the flowers. Add little dots of colour to each flower centre.

5 Glue the cake cases and leaves onto the tube stems with PVA glue. Leave to dry before putting them on your fingers.

Winter King and Queen

This finger puppet shows the king, the queen and the prince, all dressed in white fur cloaks made from fake fur. This royal family lives in a winter wonderland.

HANDY HINT

It is easier to cut fake fur on the back of the fabric than the front, especially if you need to cut an accurate shape or size. Draw your shape on the back of the fur before you start cutting.

YOU WILL NEED

Fake fur
Ruler
Scissors
Coloured card
Double-sided sticky tape
Felt-tip pen
Star stickers

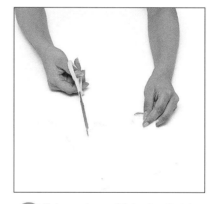

① Take a piece of fake fur that is approximately 20 cm by 10 cm. Fold the rectangle in half to make a square. Cut three holes in the folded edge big enough to push your middle three fingers through.

② For the finger puppets' heads, cut out three rectangles of card for the faces, and three differently coloured crowns. They should be wide enough to wrap around your fingers with a 1 cm overlap. Stick each face to a crown using double-sided sticky tape. Draw in the facial features.

3 Wrap the puppets' heads around each finger, peel off the paper from the double-sided sticky tape and stick firmly.

4 Stick the sides of the cloak together using double-sided sticky tape.

5 Decorate the crowns with star stickers before fitting the fur glove onto your hand. Now you are ready to push the three finger puppets onto your fingers.

Angels

A host of angels is especially appropriate to make at Christmas time. This heavenly pair look especially festive with their tinsel wings and robes edged in gold ribbon.

YOU WILL NEED

White felt
Ruler
Scissors
Gold ribbon
Double-sided sticky tape
Coloured card
PVA glue and
  glue brush
Felt-tip pens
Tinsel pipe cleaners

1 For each of the angel dresses cut out a rectangle of white felt, measuring approximately 10 cm by 12 cm. Fold over 5 cm along the long edge and cut three holes in the fold. Trim both into dress shapes. Decorate the edges by sticking on gold ribbon with double-sided sticky tape.

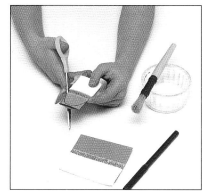

2 Cut out two rectangles of pink card 7 cm by 5 cm. Then cut out two rectangles of white felt, each 2 cm by 7 cm. Stick the felt and a strip of gold ribbon onto each pink card. Roll and stick into tubes. Draw the curved shape of the angels' heads and cut them out. Draw on the angels' faces and hair.

3 Finish the angels by sticking on haloes, cut from yellow card. Twist pipe cleaners into wing shapes and stick them on. Cut out four rectangles of white felt 4 cm by 7 cm, and trim each with a strip of ribbon. Then roll them up and stick them into tubes with double-sided sticky tape.

4 To assemble your finger puppet, put the dress on first, then the sleeves and finally the head. You will need the help of a friend or adult to put the angel on your second hand.

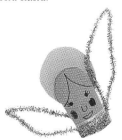

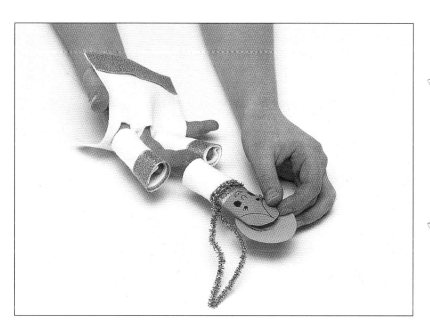

Bride and Bridesmaids

You can have great fun giving your bridesmaids different facial expressions. Here, one is in a very bad mood! Use nylon net for the bride's veil and the maids' skirts. Why not also make the groom and best man on the other hand?

YOU WILL NEED

Coloured card
Ruler
Pencil
Scissors
Coloured felt
PVA glue and glue brush
Felt-tip pens
Double-sided sticky tape
Nylon netting in
  different colours
Ribbon

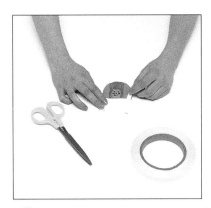

1 For the faces of the bridesmaids, cut out four rectangles of coloured card approximately 4 cm by 7 cm. Then cut out four pieces of coloured felt 2 cm by 7 cm. Glue a felt piece onto the bottom half of each piece of card. Draw the faces of the maids using felt-tip pens.

2 Fit a finger puppet around each of your first, third and fourth fingers, as well as your thumb. Stick them down using double-sided sticky tape.

3 To make the bride, cut out a rectangle of pink card 4 cm by 7 cm and trim the top edge into a curve. Draw on a face and hair with felt-tip pens. Draw and cut out a piece of white felt 7 cm by 20 cm for the bride's dress. Glue the dress onto the pink card 1 cm from edge. Trim the white felt into the shape of a dress.

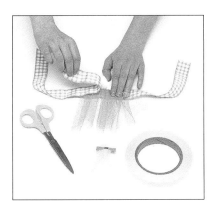

4 To make the veil, cut a piece of netting 7 cm by 7 cm and gather it into a bunch. Bind the netting with clear tape and decorate with a paper bow. For the skirt, cut a piece of netting 15 cm by 20 cm. Cut two 50 cm pieces of ribbon. Stick double-sided sticky tape along one length of ribbon. Gather the skirt onto it in the middle. Stick the second piece of ribbon over the top.

5 Now tie the ribbon around your hand to attach the skirt. Slip the bridesmaids over your fingers and thumb. Finally, add the bride. Don't forget her veil!

27

Fishermen and Fishing Net

This puppet shows a group of fishermen in their waterproof fishing coats and hoods. They have caught a lot of fish, including one that looks suspiciously like a shark, so let's hope they're strong enough to haul it in! Fishnet tights make a great net, and rubber gloves are perfect for waterproof coats.

YOU WILL NEED
Coloured card
Pencil
Scissors
Dot stickers
Felt-tip pen
Fishnet tights
Sticky tape
Pair of washing-up gloves
Glue stick

1 Fold a piece of orange card into about six layers. Draw a fish on the top layer and cut it out. Draw and cut out a shark shape from a different colour of card.

2 Decorate the fish cut-outs with dot stickers for eyes. Draw in the eyes and teeth of the shark in felt-tip pen.

3 Draw and cut out a net shape from white card. Slip the card into one of the feet of the fishnet tights. Cut off the tights at the top of the card and tape down at the back.

28

4 Cut off the four fingers of one of the washing-up gloves, so that they are still all joined at the bottom. Cut off the four fingertips from the other glove.

5 Cut out four coloured card circles and draw a bearded fisherman's face on each. Cut a little round hole in one side of each glove fingertip to make a hood. Put on the glove fingers and slip a hood onto each finger. Stick on the faces to look as if they are peeping out of the hoods. Add dot stickers to make bold buttons down the front of the raincoats. Glue the fish onto the net. Glue and tape the net onto the front edge of the glove.

29

Animals in the Forest

On one hand, your fingers are a forest and on the other hand, you have all the forest animals. When you put your hands together, you can see a fox, a wolf, a tiger and a badger peeking through the trees!

YOU WILL NEED

Coloured card
Ruler
Pencil
Scissors
Acrylic paints
Paintbrush
Double-sided sticky tape
Cotton wool
Glue stick
PVA glue and glue brush
Kitchen cloth
Face paints
Make-up brush

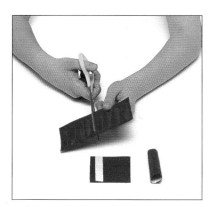

1 Cut four rectangles of card 5 cm by 7 cm each, for the tree trunks. Paint on stripes for the bark. Stick a piece of double-sided sticky tape down one side edge of each piece. Wrap and stick the card tubes around your fingers.

2 Now cut four treetop shapes from coloured card and glue a wad of cotton wool to each with a glue stick. Paint each wad with green acrylic paint and leave to dry.

3 Glue the tree tops to the tree trunk tubes with PVA glue and leave to dry.

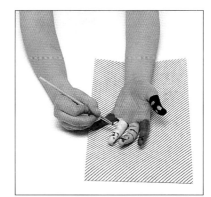

HANDY HINT

Cotton wool makes really great fluffy trees. You can buy several different kinds in most chemists, but the most useful kind comes in a roll.

4 Over a kitchen cloth, paint the animals onto the fingers of your other hand. Use face paints and a make-up brush. Remember to clean the brush before using different colours of paints. Leave each colour to dry on your skin before applying a new one.

31

Octopus

With the help of face and body paints you can use your fingers to make the tentacles of an octopus. Paint your palm to look like suction pads on the underside of the octopus tentacles.

YOU WILL NEED
Kitchen cloth
Face paints
Make-up sponge
Make-up brush

HANDY HINT
Always clean your brush and sponge between colours, otherwise the paint colours will mix together. Also, if you use a towel or flannel instead of a kitchen cloth, make sure it is an old one so that it doesn't matter if it gets stained.

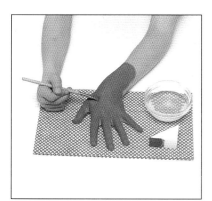

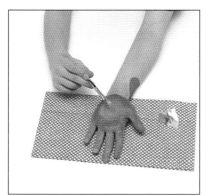

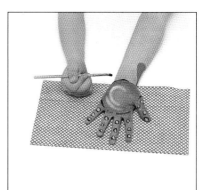

1 Lay a kitchen cloth on your work surface. Apply blue face paint to your hand with a make-up sponge. Leave to dry for a few minutes, then add another layer with a make-up brush. Leave to dry.

2 Turn your hand over and paint the palm pink. To get a good pink colour, mix red and white face paints on a sponge and apply the first layer to your skin. Apply a second layer with a make-up brush.

3 With the make-up brush, paint white dots on your fingers. Leave to dry for a few minutes. Outline the white dots with a fine line of black face paint. Leave to dry.

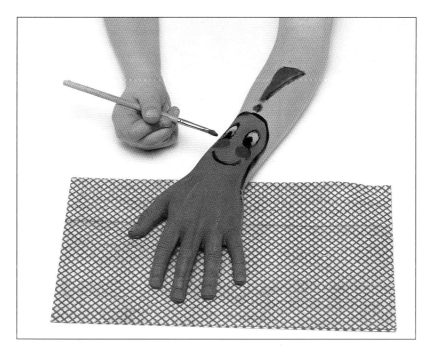

4 Turn over your hand and paint the face of the octopus onto the blue background.

Painted Stag

This painted hand puppet captures the elegant beauty of a proud stag. The shape is made using the little finger and first finger as horns and the two middle fingers and thumb as a nose and mouth. The stag's magnificent antlers and eye are cut from coloured card.

YOU WILL NEED
Kitchen cloth
Face paints
Make-up sponge
Make-up brush
Scissors
Coloured card
Pencil
Masking tape
Glue stick

1 Rest your hand on a kitchen cloth and apply a coat of brown face paint with a make-up sponge. Leave to dry then add a coat of lighter brown paint on top using a make-up brush.

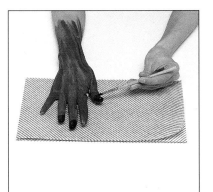

2 Using a make-up brush, paint the ends of your thumb and two middle fingers black.

3 Pinch your fingers together to make a stag shape. Paint the eye outline using white paint. Then paint a black line around it and a row of eyelashes.

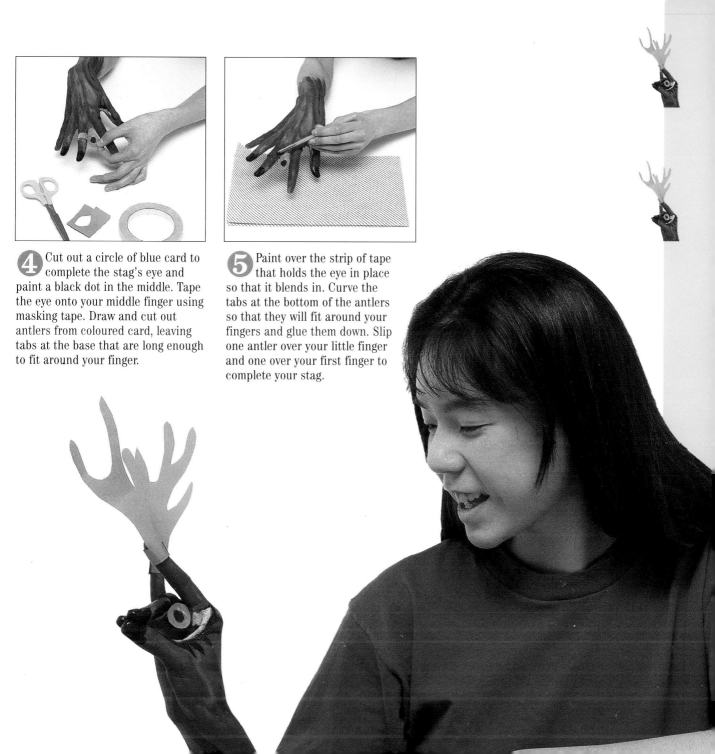

4 Cut out a circle of blue card to complete the stag's eye and paint a black dot in the middle. Tape the eye onto your middle finger using masking tape. Draw and cut out antlers from coloured card, leaving tabs at the base that are long enough to fit around your finger.

5 Paint over the strip of tape that holds the eye in place so that it blends in. Curve the tabs at the bottom of the antlers so that they will fit around your fingers and glue them down. Slip one antler over your little finger and one over your first finger to complete your stag.

Footballer

This is a favourite with sports fans. Use your fingers as legs and see if you can score with the ball. Think of other ways to use your fingers as legs and then experiment with hand painting – you could make a can-can dancer.

YOU WILL NEED
Kitchen cloth
Face paints
Make-up sponge
Make-up brush
Table tennis ball
Acrylic paints
Paintbrush

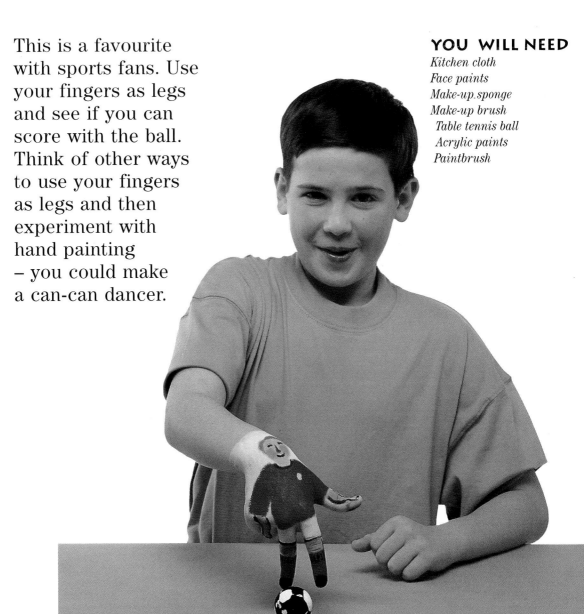

1 Lay the kitchen cloth on your work surface. Apply a base coat of white face paint to one hand with a make-up sponge. Leave to dry.

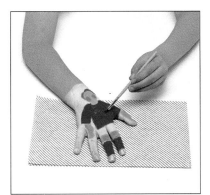

2 Paint on the red socks and shirt with the make-up brush. Paint the face, arms and knees a different colour from the base coat. Leave to dry for a few minutes.

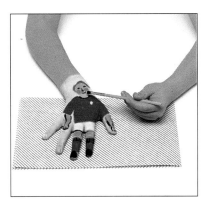

3 Paint a black outline around the footballer. Now you can paint in his black boots and facial features.

4 Paint a table tennis ball with black acrylic paint. When the paint has dried, carefully add the white markings you find on a football. World Cup finger puppet football, here we come!

Little Devil

We can use our hands and fingers to make all sorts of shapes and creatures, including this little devil. Face paints, a cloak and a fork complete the illusion. The first and fourth fingers form the devil's horns and the two middle fingers are curled over to make the hair.

YOU WILL NEED

Kitchen cloth
Face paints
Make-up sponge
Make-up brush
Gold glitter gel
Scissors
Nylon netting
Black paper
PVA glue and
  glue brush

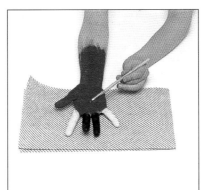

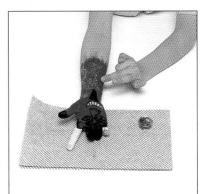

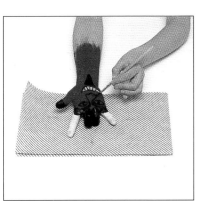

1 Lay down a kitchen cloth and apply a layer of red paint to your hand, wrist and thumb with a make-up sponge. Paint your first finger and little finger white and your two middle fingers black. Cover any patches in the red paint using the make-up brush.

2 When the base colours have dried, use black and white paint and a make-up brush to add the little devil's eyes, nose, teeth and beard.

3 Gently smear gold glitter gel over the red paint on your wrist to make the devil's neck glint and shimmer.

4 Cut a length of red netting. Ask a friend to help you to tie it around your wrist to make a cloak. Cut a fork from black paper and glue it to the front of the devil's cloak.

Waltzing Couple

Transform your socks into a couple of dancers. You can dress the woman in a wonderful boa, and the man in a top hat and bow tie.

YOU WILL NEED

Two socks in different colours
Scissors
Ruler
Coloured felt
Coloured card
Double-sided sticky tape
Red pencil

Scrap paper
PVA glue and glue brush
Felt-tip pens
Ribbon
Needle
Thread
Feather trim

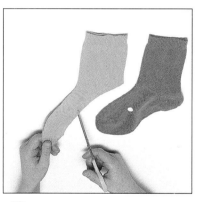

1 Fold each sock lengthways and cut a small hole about halfway between the toe and the heel. This will make a hole on each side of the sock. The hole should be big enough to fit your thumb.

2 Cut out four rectangles of felt, approximately 5 cm by 7 cm. Draw four arms on card and cut them out. Stick an arm in the centre of each felt rectangle with double-sided sticky tape. Stick double-sided sticky tape down one side edge of each rectangle. Draw nails on the hands with a red pencil, then roll up and stick each sleeve around the finger you will wear it on.

3 To make the woman's hair, draw around your three middle fingers on a piece of scrap paper. Make the bottom edge straight, and draw a curve around the top, about 1 cm away from the ends of your fingers. Cut out and use the paper as a template for cutting two pieces of felt. Cut a semicircle from the bottom of a felt piece. Glue three of the sides together to make a pouch.

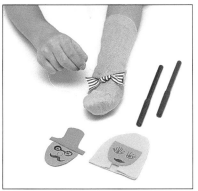

4 Cut out two faces from coloured card and draw on the features with felt-tip pens. Stick the woman's face onto her hair and decorate the man's face with a hat cut from card. Make a bow tie for the man by tying a 20 cm length of ribbon into a bow. Sew it onto one of the socks, then stick it on the man's face.

5 Assemble the puppets by putting your hands into the socks and then placing the woman's head over the top of one of the socks. Push a finger through each hole in the side of the sock and slip the arms onto your fingers. Finally, drape the woman sock with approximately 50 cm of feather trim for the boa.

Big Beaky Bird

This puppet is very simple to make, but amazingly expressive. You operate the beak by putting your thumb in the lower beak and your fingers in the upper beak. With a little practice, you can pick up things as well. By moving your arm and wrist, the bird can look shy, sleepy, hungry, happy, or just plain mad!

YOU WILL NEED

Compass
Pencil
Ruler
Coloured card
Scissors
Double-sided sticky tape
PVA glue and glue brush
Coloured crêpe paper
Black sticky tape
Black pop sock

1 First, make two cones for the upper and lower beaks. Use a compass, a pencil and a ruler to draw two semicircles on coloured card. Draw one with a 15 cm radius and the other with a 10 cm radius. Cut them out, leaving a tab 2 cm by 3 cm on the smaller semicircle.

2 Roll each semicircle into a cone and stick them together with double-sided sticky tape. Stick the tab on the smaller cone inside the larger cone to hold the upper and lower beaks together.

3 To make the bird's plume, fold and glue some yellow crêpe paper into a fan shape and glue strips of orange crêpe paper onto the front.

4 Cut out two white card ovals and two smaller blue circles. Glue them together to make the eyes. Glue the eyes inside the top of the beak and hold tightly for a couple of minutes. Glue the plume inside the top of the beak. Use black sticky tape to make the pupils and nostrils.

5 Cut a hole in the pop sock that is large enough to put your thumb through. Put the sock on by placing your thumb into the bottom of the beak and your fingers into the upper part.

Goofy Horse

One of the simplest ways to make a glove puppet is to use a mitten. The teeth and eyes give this horse puppet a really daft look.

YOU WILL NEED

Darning needle
Wool
Mitten
Ruler
Scissors
Felt-tip pen
Coloured cartridge paper
Pipe cleaners
PVA glue and glue brush
White card
Double-sided sticky tape

1 First, make the mane of your horse. Thread the darning needle with wool and make a stitch at the end of the mitten. Leave a loop approximately 5 cm long, then make a tight stitch. Repeat this in a line up the mitten and finish off with a knot. Cut the end of each loop to make a shaggy mane.

2 Draw the ears and eyes on cartridge paper and cut them out. Each eye is made up of the lid, a blue circle for the eyeball, and 1 cm of pipe cleaner glued on with PVA glue for the eyelash. Allow plenty of time for the glue to dry.

3 Draw a row of teeth, approximately 5 cm long, on a piece of white card using a felt-tip pen. Draw three tabs, two small and one large, along the top of the row of teeth. Cut out the teeth and the tabs.

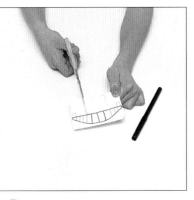

4 Form the teeth into a curve by sticking the two small tabs to the large one with double-sided sticky tape.

5 Put the mitten on. Glue or tape the eyes and teeth onto the mitten and leave to dry. Finally, attach pipe cleaner reins.

Mermaid

This fun glove puppet is made from a woollen sock. She's a rather glamorous mermaid and her tail and bikini top are decorated with shimmering sequins. You could also glue on buttons, bits of foil or other shiny material to make her sparkle even more! Her lustrous hair and her face are added to the sock with coloured wool.

YOU WILL NEED

Cardboard
Scissors
Sock
Coloured wools
Darning needle
Ruler
Pencil
Coloured card
Nylon netting
PVA glue and glue brush
Sequins

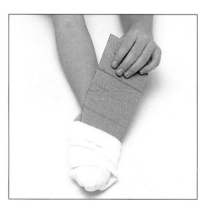

1 Cut a long cardboard rectangle with a curve at one end. Push the card inside the sock to keep the two sides apart while you sew.

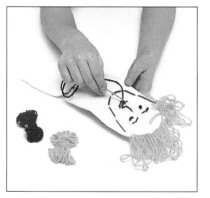

2 Using yellow wool and a darning needle, sew 8 cm loops along the top of the sock to make the mermaid's hair. After every loop, make a small stitch to keep it in place. Sew the mermaid's features using different coloured wools for the eyes, mouth and nose.

3 Draw the mermaid's tail on blue card and cut it out. Cut a piece of nylon netting and glue it to the tail. Make the net slightly crumpled. Cut a bikini top from red card. Use PVA glue to stick sequins to the front of the tail and the bikini top as decoration.

HANDY HINT
*If you don't have any
sequins, you can always
use glitter – your mermaid
will shimmer just as well!*

4 Glue the tail onto the sock and glue the bikini top above the tail. Leave to dry.

Sock Serpent

This bright red snake puppet is made from a pair of tights, so it covers your whole arm when it is worn. The snake has an enormous forked tongue. Did you know that snakes use their tongues to smell instead of noses?

YOU WILL NEED
Pair of woollen tights
Scissors
Pencil
Card
Double-sided sticky tape
Felt-tip pen
Wool
Darning needle
Coloured felt
PVA glue and glue brush
Beads

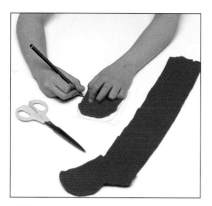

1 Cut one leg from the tights. It should be long enough to cover your whole arm. Cut the foot from the other leg of the tights just below the heel. Draw around this foot on thin card and cut out.

2 Turn the foot inside out. Turn over the raw edges of the foot and use double-sided sticky tape to stick them down. Turn the foot the right way out again and slide in the card to stiffen it.

3 Pull the snake's body over your arm. Mark where your thumb is with a felt-tip pen, remove the snake and cut a small hole for your thumb. This will allow you to move the lower half of the snake's mouth when it is in place. Using wool and a darning needle, sew the top edge of the lower mouth to the main body of the snake, just above the hole for your thumb.

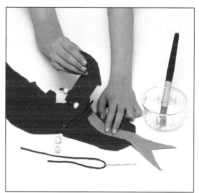

4 Cut a forked tongue from felt and glue it inside the snake's mouth. Stitch a bead to either side of the top of the snake's head to make its eyes. Cut two small semicircles of felt and glue them above the eyes to make the eyebrows.

Elephant

This glove puppet is made from a pair of grey woollen socks. Slip your fingers up the back of the elephant's head and use your thumb to make the mouth. When you move your thumb up and down to close the mouth, the trunk moves up and down as well.

YOU WILL NEED

Pair of grey, ribbed knee socks
Scissors
Plastic tubing
Wool
Darning needle
Buttons
Needle
Thread
Pencil
Coloured card
Double-sided sticky tape
Round bath sponge

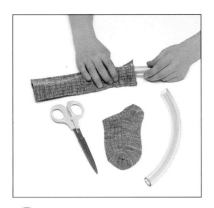

1 Cut one sock in half, just above the heel. The long part of the sock will make the elephant's trunk. Cut a piece of plastic tubing to the same length and place it inside the long part of the sock.

2 Pull the sock tightly around the tube. Stitch the sock together halfway along its length using wool and a darning needle. Now the tube is held firmly in place.

3 Sew a button on each side of the foot of the other sock to make the elephant's eyes. Cut a small hole in the heel, large enough to slip your thumb through. Use wool and a darning needle to stitch the trunk opening to the sock just above the hole.

4 For the elephant's ears, cut the foot left over from the first sock into two pieces. Draw and cut out two ear shapes from coloured card, using the two sock pieces as a guide. Stick a sock piece onto each piece of card with double-sided tape and trim the sock to fit the card.

5 Cut the bath sponge in two and stuff one half up the elephant to pad out the face. Now attach the ears, first with double-sided sticky tape to hold them in place, and then with a darning needle and wool to stitch them on more securely.

Happy Woman, Blue Man

A fun variation on the glove puppet is the foot puppet. Socks have never been so bizarre! Here, each foot represents a different mood, with a happy, smiling woman in pink and a rather sad man in blue. They're lots of fun, so why not make lots for all your friends?

YOU WILL NEED

Card
Scissors
Two socks in different colours
Coloured felt
Glue stick
Needle
Thread
Ribbon
Beads or buttons

1 Cut out two pieces of card and slide one inside each sock. The card needs to be slightly larger than the sock, so that the sock stretches.

2 Cut out features for the sock faces from felt – lips, cheeks, eyes, nose, eyebrows, hair and a bow. Give each sock a different expression. Glue the felt features onto the bottom of each sock.

3 Sew the middle of a piece of ribbon to the back of the happy woman sock. Sew on beads or buttons for extra decoration.

4 Try on the happy woman sock, and tie the ribbon so that it fits with your foot inside it.

Peacock Glove Puppet

Peacocks fan out their beautiful feathers to impress the peahens. With this glove puppet you can open and close your fingers to mimic the movement of the bird.

YOU WILL NEED

Ruler
Fabric glove
Coloured card
Felt-tip pen
Scissors
Coloured felt
PVA glue and glue brush
Sequins

1 Measure the length of the middle finger of the glove and add 2 cm. Fold a piece of coloured card into five layers and draw a feather shape to that measurement. Cut out the feathers.

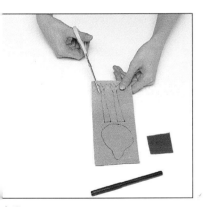

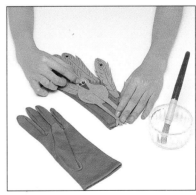

2 Now measure the glove from the opening to the base of the fingers. Draw the body and legs of the peacock on felt to fit inside the glove measurement. On a small piece of pink or red felt, draw and cut out the beak. Stick the legs to the body and the beak to the face.

3 Decorate the feathers using the felt-tip pen. Gently dab the sequins with some PVA glue and stick them onto the feathers. Glue another two sequins onto the bird face for the eyes.

4 Glue the bird and feathers onto the glove and leave plenty of time to dry. It's a good idea to slip some card into the glove so that the glue doesn't seep through the fabric.

Traditional Puppet Theatre

This fun box has the red curtain and bare board stage of a traditional theatre. It is made from a large, thin box and decorated using brightly coloured paper and paints. Why not add your own bits of scenery for each show?

YOU WILL NEED
Cardboard box
Ruler
Coloured paper
Glue stick
Craft knife
Cutting mat
Acrylic paint and paintbrush
Pencil
Scissors
Ribbon

1 Take a cardboard box that is approximately 30 cm by 50 cm. Cover the bottom of the box with brightly coloured paper using a glue stick. Smooth the paper with the palm of your hand to flatten any bubbles. Paint the sides of the box with black acrylic paint. Allow to dry.

2 Fold out one long side of the box to make the floor of the theatre. Draw the curtains inside the bottom of the box – draw one curtain on each side. Ask an adult to cut along the lines with a craft knife, remembering to use a cutting mat to protect the work surface.

3 Paint the stage floor of your theatre in big bold stripes. You can do this without a ruler as the effect isn't supposed to be perfect.

4 Stick decorative ribbon onto the front of the theatre curtain using the glue stick. Now you can put on a show for all your friends.

Forest Theatre Box

Your finger puppet character can wander through an enchanted woodland once you have made this theatre. You can add a large yellow sun for a daytime scene or a shining silver moon for night.

YOU WILL NEED
Cardboard box
Scissors
White card
Pencil
Ruler
Craft knife
Cutting mat
Coloured paper
Glue stick
PVA glue and glue brush
Fake grass
Masking tape
Glitter

1 Cut off the lid flaps from the box using a pair of scissors. Then place the box on a piece of white card and draw around it.

2 With a ruler and pencil, draw over the box outline so that it is clear and straight. Draw a tree-shaped border inside the outline.

3 Ask an adult to cut out the tree-shaped border using a craft knife, working on a cutting mat. Make sure you keep the basic square shape intact. This will form the front of the theatre.

4 Draw around the outline of the trees on a piece of green paper. Cut it out and stick it on top of the white card using the glue stick. Cut out a yellow sun shape and stick it on with PVA glue.

5 Cover the outside of the box with coloured paper and glue the fake grass onto the stage floor. Glue the front of the stage to the theatre box and hold in place with masking tape while the glue dries. Dab PVA glue onto the front of the stage and sprinkle with glitter. Catch any surplus glitter on a piece of clean paper to use another time.

HANDY HINT

Ask your local green-grocer if he or she has any spare scraps of fake grass. If you can't get hold of any, you could always use green felt.

59

South American Bus

Finger puppets work really well with a piece of scenery. Attach this bus to your hand with elastic and use your other hand to work the finger puppets. Buses in South America often travel long distances from town to town and are decorated with brightly coloured stripes.

1 Draw a bus shape on card and cut it out. Carefully draw around the bus onto coloured paper and cut it out.

2 For the wheels, cover two used sticky tape rolls with coloured tape. Draw around the tape rolls on brightly coloured paper. Cut out the two circles and stick one onto the front of each wheel using PVA glue.

3 Glue the coloured paper onto the card bus using a glue stick. Cut a strip of coloured paper to run along the roof of the bus and glue it on. Then glue on the wheels with PVA glue. Leave to dry for at least 15 minutes. Decorate the bus with strips of coloured tape. This is easiest if you stick on a strip of tape which is a bit longer than the bus and then trim it to fit.

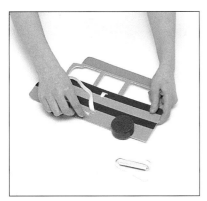

HANDY HINT

When buying the white card ask for some that is thin enough to cut with scissors, yet stiff enough to stand up straight.

4 Carefully make four slits in the bus, beneath the middle window, using a pair of scissors. Thread the elastic through the slits, pulling it flat, as it will stretch when you put your hand in it. Tie it in a knot at the back.

Sailing Boat

This prop is perfect to use with the fishermen and fishing net puppet. Why not make a story with your friends to include the octopus and the mermaid, too?

YOU WILL NEED

Compass
Pencil
Stiff card
Scissors
Coloured paper
Glue stick
String
PVA glue and
 glue brush
Wooden barbeque
 skewer or garden
 stick
Elastic

1 Use a compass and pencil to draw a semicircle on a piece of stiff card. Cut it out. Draw around the shape on two pieces of paper, one red and one blue, then cut out. Draw a wavy line near the top of the blue outline and another near the bottom. Cut along the two lines and discard the middle strip.

2 Stick the bottom section of the blue paper onto the card boat. Now stick the top strip of blue paper onto the middle of the boat. Leave some white card visible for the froth of the waves. Cut a wavy line halfway down the red boat shape and stick the top section to the top of the card boat. Wrap string round the top of the boat, to look like a rope. Glue the string to the back of the boat.

3 While the glue is drying, cut a triangular sail shape from coloured paper. Tape it onto the wooden barbeque skewer or garden stick. Ask an adult to trim any sharp ends on the skewer.

4 Cut four small slits in the centre of the boat. Thread the elastic through and tie at the back. You now have a handle that you can slip onto your hand.

ACKNOWLEDGEMENTS

The Publishers would like to thank the following children
for modelling for this book, and their parents for making
it possible for them to do so:

Kirsty Fraser
Sophia Groome
Nicholas Lie
Tania Murphy
Kim Peterson
Mai-Anh Peterson
Alexandra Richards
Leigh Richards
Alex Simons
Antonino Sipiano
Maria Tsang